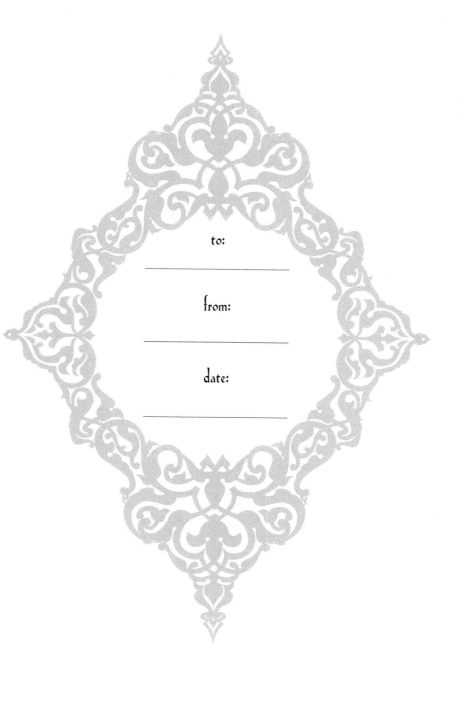

to:
_____

from:

_____

date:

_____

Owner's Manual

The Essential Guide to the One You Love

Arielle Ford and Elizabeth Goodman

JODERE
GROUP
San Diego, California

JODERE

GROUP

JODERE GROUP, INC.
P.O. Box 910147
San Diego, CA 92191-0147
800.569.1002
www.jodere.com

CIP data available from the Library of Congress

ISBN 1-58872-032-2
05 04 03 02   4 3 2 1
First printing, October 2002

Book cover and interior design by CHARLES MCSTRAVICK
Editorial supervision by CHAD EDWARDS

PRINTED IN THE UNITED STATES OF AMERICA

This book is dedicated to

Herb Tanzer

Contents

Introduction

All major appliances, cars, and computers come with an owner's manual. Often, it's a step-by-step guide that tells us how to turn it on, turn it off, and how to fix it when it's broken. Imagine if your soul mate came with such a manual—the complete instruction guide to the lifetime care and operation of the one you love—a guide that told you how, when, and where to make all their dreams come true. That is exactly what this book is meant to be—the complete guide to the one you love.

Elizabeth is a woman to whom the little details mean a lot. You can totally make her day by giving her a greeting card embellished with words of love and appreciation. Her husband, Herb, wasn't quite getting it. He was sure she was perfectly happy just "knowing" how much he loved her. Finally, out of shear frustration, Elizabeth decided to make a little "owner's manual" for Herb so that he would have explicit directions on how to keep her smiling. The result? Herb was thrilled to have directions and Elizabeth got what she needed to feel loved, cherished, and adored.

As soon as I heard about this idea I just knew the *world* was ready for it. Elizabeth and I agreed to team up to bring forth the very first *Owner's Manual* for lovers. Ideally, you will buy two copies—one for you and one for your beloved. It doesn't matter if you've just started dating or have been married for years—there are always new and surprising facts to learn about each other's wants, needs, desires and fantasies. Complete and exchange manuals. Then make a date, open a bottle of wine, light a fire, and snuggle close while you explore each other's books and discover the things that will take your lover to bliss.

We wish you love, happiness and fun surprises!

Arielle Ford
&
Elizabeth Goodman

History

Name on my birth certificate _____

Name I go by _____

Date of birth _____

    Time _____

    City _____

    State _____

Height _____

Weight _____

Hair color _____

Eye color _____

Significant birth events _____

Mother's maiden name _____

Father's name _____

Sisters & brothers names _____

_____

_____

Nicknames _____

_____

_____

Favorite childhood toys _____

Favorite things to do when I was little included _____

_____

_____

Kindergarten I attended _____

Elementary School _____

Significant Childhood Events _____

_____

_____

_____

Jr. High School _____

High School _____

    Extracurricular Activities _____

    _____

    _____

    Sports played _____

    _____

_____

Awards _____

_____

Prom Date _____

    I wore _____

    _____

    It was held at _____

College _____

Favorite subjects in school _____

_____

_____

_____

_____

Religious Activities (baptism, bar mitzvah, etc.) _____

_____

_____

_____

_____

_____

_____

Family & Pets

Today my family consists of:

wife/husband _____

children (and ages) _____

_____

_____

ex's _____

sisters _____

_____

brothers _____

_____

parents _____

grandparents _____

aunts & uncles _____

_____

_____

cousins _____

_____

_____

others _____

I am _____ close to my family.

My favorite relative is _____

. . . because _____

_____

_____

My favorite animal is _____

The first pet I ever owned was a _____

Ideally, I would like to have _____ pets.

They would include _____

_____

I would not like to have a _____

. . . because _____

_____

_____

Friends

My very best friend is _____

Some of my other friends are _____

_____

_____

The friend that is most like family is _____

_____

My funniest friend is _____

My smartest friend is _____

My oldest friend that I am still in touch with is _____

My friend that lives farthest away is _____

The qualities, which are very important to me in a friend are _____

_____

_____

_____

My friends come to me for _____

_____

    . . . and that makes me feel _____

_____

_____

I have lost friends because _____

_____

_____

Things I like to do with one friend are _____

_____

_____

_____

Things I like to do with a group of friends are _____

_____

_____

_____

_____

Of all my childhood friends that I have lost contact with, the one I would most like

to see again is _____

   . . . because _____

_____

_____

_____

_____

_____

Health

I am _____ healthy.

My best health habit is _____

The least healthy thing I do is _____

Exercises I enjoy _____
_____

Exercises I dislike _____
_____

I exercise _____ times a week

Vitamins & supplements I take daily _____
_____

I am allergic to _____
_____

    . . . my reaction is _____
_____

The health problem(s) I have _____
_____
_____
_____
_____

The medication(s) I must take _____

My family has a history of _____

I expect to live to the age of _____
Illnesses I have had _____

When I get sick it is usually because of _____

I have been admitted to a hospital _____ times.
    I was admitted for _____

My health insurance carrier is _____

Care & Maintenance

Morning rituals _____

_____

Bedtime rituals _____

_____

I require _____ hours of sleep per night.

If I don't get that amount this is what happens _____

_____

I like to sleep on the _____ side of the bed

I need _____ pillows, preferably _____

I like to sleep with the windows _____

   . . . and the air conditioning/heater _____

The way I like to fall asleep is _____

_____

The way I like to be awakened is _____

_____

If I wake up in the middle of the night from a nightmare, please _____

_____

_____

I like to take _____ showers/baths per day.

This is an activity that I _____ prefer to do alone.

I prefer the following accoutrements with my bathing _____

_____

_____

My favorite toothpaste is _____

Body parts I most enjoy having massaged are _____

_____

_____

_____

Feeding Requirements

I need to eat _____ times a day.

Preferably at the following times _____

_____

If I miss a meal I get _____

My favorite:

breakfast foods are _____

_____

lunch foods are _____

_____

dinner foods are _____

_____

meal of the day is _____

desserts are _____

_____

alcoholic/non-alcoholic beverages are _____

_____

kind of sweets _____

_____

_____

restaurants _____

_____

_____

fast food places _____

_____

_____

comfort foods are _____

_____

. . . because _____

_____

Cooking to me is _____

_____

My specialties include _____

_____

_____

I hate the following foods _____

_____

I'm allergic to these foods _____

_____

I often crave these foods _____

_____

_____

... especially when _____

_____

_____

Foods that give me gas _____

_____

_____

What Makes Me, Me!

My astrological sign is _____

I am typical of my sign because I have these traits _____
_____

I am not typical of my sign because _____
_____
_____

The thing that makes me different from most people is _____
_____
_____
_____

Something people may not know about me is _____
_____
_____
_____

Something I would like people to understand about me is _____
_____
_____
_____
_____

My phobias and superstitions are _____

_____

_____

_____

People and things that scare me _____

_____

_____

_____

People and things that make me laugh _____

_____

_____

_____

Something I would never do is _____

_____

_____

Something I've always wanted to do is _____

_____

_____

_____

The event that has had the most significance in my life was _____

_____

_____

_____

_____

The person that has had the most significance in my life is/was _____

_____

_____

The best way to get me to do something I don't want to do is _____

_____

_____

I was _____ when I left home.

I went to _____

_____

_____

I learned how to drive when I was _____ years old.

I was taught by _____

It was a _____ experience.

Generally I am a _____ driver.

I consider my traffic record to be _____

When I'm in heavy traffic, I generally get _____

When someone else drives, I feel very _____

My most precious possession _____
_____

The one thing I've always wanted, but never gotten is _____
_____
_____
_____
_____

Tattoos I have and where they are located _____
_____
_____

Piercings I have and where they are located _____
_____

I have played "hookie" from school/work/life to _____
_____
_____

Social Views

I _____ believe one person can make a difference.

I think the most important social issues on the planet today are _____

_____

_____

_____

If I were in charge, this is what I would do about them _____

_____

_____

_____

_____

This is what I am doing about them now _____

_____

_____

The charities to which I contribute time and/or money are _____

_____

_____

_____

I think the most significant differences between men and women are _____

_____

_____

_____

_____

The transformational/motivational seminars I have attended are _____

_____

_____

Service organizations I belong to _____

_____

Professional organizations I belong to include _____

_____

My thoughts on euthanasia are _____

_____

_____

Things I Think About

If I could have the world my way I would _____

_____

_____

_____

_____

_____

If I had $20 million I would spend it on _____

_____

_____

_____

_____

If I could meet one person, dead or alive, it would be _____

_____

   . . . because _____

_____

_____

_____

_____

_____

If I were famous, this is what I would want to be famous for _____

_____

_____

_____

_____

If I could have any three wishes they would be _____

_____

_____

_____

_____

_____

_____

_____

_____

_____

_____

_____

_____

_____

_____

Upsets & Moods

I have a _____ temper.

The early warning signs that I am angry include _____

_____

_____

_____

_____

The worst possible things to do or say when I'm angry are _____

_____

_____

_____

_____

Techniques I use to calm myself down _____

_____

_____

Things that make me cry _____

_____

_____

_____

_____

The best way to help me when I am:

angry _____

_____

sad _____

_____

depressed _____

_____

moody _____

_____

I need to be hugged _____ times a day.

Ten things that can get me in a good mood:

1. _____
2. _____
3. _____
4. _____
5. _____
6. _____
7. _____
8. _____

9. _____

10. _____

Ten things that can get me in a bad mood:

1. _____

2. _____

3. _____

4. _____

5. _____

6. _____

7. _____

8. _____

9. _____

10. _____

Alone Time

These are the things I really enjoy doing when I have time all to myself:

1. _____

2. _____

3. _____

4. _____

5. _____

6. _____

7. _____

8. _____

9. _____

10. _____

My Perfect Day

I would wake up at _____

The first thing I would do is _____

Then spend the rest of the day _____

_____

_____

_____

_____

I would like to spend the day with _____

In the early evening I would _____

_____

_____

The last thing I would do before going to bed is _____

_____

_____

I would sleep with _____

   . . . and dream about _____

_____

_____

_____

Saturdays & Sundays

On Saturdays I _____ have a routine that I follow.

On Saturdays I like to _____

_____

_____

_____

_____

My idea of the perfect Saturday night is _____

_____

_____

_____

_____

_____

On Sundays I _____ have a routine that I follow.

On Sundays I like to _____

_____

_____

_____

_____

_____

My idea of the perfect Sunday is _____

_____

_____

_____

_____

_____

_____

_____

_____

My idea of a heavenly weekend is to _____

_____

_____

_____

_____

_____

_____

_____

_____

_____

Career

When I was a child, I dreamt of becoming a _____

_____

_____

The first job I ever had _____

The best job I ever had _____

The worst job I ever had _____

The job I would never want to do is _____

My major accomplishments include _____

_____

_____

_____

My biggest failure was _____

_____

_____

_____

Currently I earn my living as _____

_____

What I love most about it is _____

_____

What frustrates me most about it is _____

_____

The one thing I would most like to change about my situation is _____

_____

_____

_____

If I had to do it all over again I would _____

_____

_____

_____

_____

_____

_____

_____

_____

My dream career is to _____

_____

_____

_____

Money

I am _____ with money.

I grew up in a _____ home and the main lesson I learned about money was

_____

_____

_____

I tend to spend money _____

My attitude toward money is _____

_____

_____

I currently have the following monetary accounts/sources: _____

_____

_____

_____

_____

I have _____ credit cards.

I pay my bills _____

I stick to a budget _____

I balance my checkbook _____

My credit rating is _____

I _____ prefer to handle my own finances.

My outstanding debts include _____

_____

_____

_____

My views on lending money to a friend _____

_____

_____

_____

When asked by a transient for money, I usually _____

_____

_____

I _____ know my net worth.

Music & Books

Types of music I like _____

_____

_____

Music that inspires me _____

Music I like to dance to _____

Music I grew up on _____

_____

The song that brings back the most memories _____

Songs I find myself singing in the shower _____

_____

_____

My musical abilities consist of _____

_____

_____

If I could play any instrument it would be _____

   ... because _____

_____

The best concert I ever went to see was _____

_____

Someday I would like to see _____

_____

The types of books I like to read are _____

_____

The best book I ever read was _____

Worst book I ever read _____

   . . . because _____

_____

_____

_____

The book that changed me was _____

   . . . because _____

_____

_____

_____

My views on lending books _____

_____

_____

_____

Music & Books

My favorite:

musicians are _____

_____

_____

_____

soundtrack/CD is _____

authors are _____

_____

_____

_____

time to read is _____

place to read _____

book to recommend _____

fairytale _____

classic _____

Movies & Television

Types of movies I like _____

_____

Please don't take me to any _____ movies.

Funniest movie I ever saw _____

Scariest movie I ever saw _____

Worst movie I ever saw _____

Movies that bring a smile _____

_____

Movies that make me cry _____

_____

If someone were to play me in a movie it would be _____

. . . because _____

Types of shows I can't stand _____

_____

Shows I grew up watching were _____

_____

_____

TV character I am most like _____

I like to watch TV in the _____ room.

I like to eat _____ while I'm watching TV.

My views on the remote control _____

_____

_____

_____

I _____ fall asleep with the TV on.

My favorite:

movies _____

_____

_____

_____

_____

_____

movie stars are _____

_____

_____

_____

_____

_____

_____

theater is _____

snacks at the theater are _____

TV shows are _____

_____

_____

_____

_____

morning show is _____

talk show host is _____

sit-com is _____

mini-series was _____

Sports & Games

The activity I'm best at is _____

_____

_____

_____

_____

Games I like to play _____

_____

Sports and activities I don't like are _____

_____

My favorite:

sports to participate in are _____

_____

sports to watch are _____

_____

athlete _____

leisure activities are _____

_____

_____

_____

physical activities are _____

_____

_____

_____

_____

Shopping

My favorite:

city to shop in is _____

mall is _____

stores to shop in are _____

_____

_____

_____

_____

catalogs are _____

_____

_____

designers _____

_____

colors for clothes _____

_____

sleepwear _____

fragrances _____

Fabrics I love _____

_____

Fabrics I dislike _____

I like clothes that are _____

My oldest piece of clothing is _____

I love it because _____

My sizes are:

_____ dress/suit

_____ blouse/shirt

_____ pants

_____ shoe

_____ socks/pantihose

_____ underwear

_____ bathing suit

_____ hat

_____ ring

Things I Like

My absolute favorite thing in the world is _____

_____

_____

_____

My favorite:

color _____

sounds _____

smell _____

gemstones _____

flowers _____

trees _____

collectibles _____

car _____

words _____

quote _____

_____

_____

day of the week _____

season _____

The best way to surprise me:

at work _____

_____

_____

when I get home _____

_____

_____

on the weekends _____

_____

_____

on my birthday _____

_____

_____

for no reason at all _____

_____

_____

Things I Don't Like

Sounds _____

Smells _____

Words _____

Colors _____

People that do _____

_____

_____

People that say _____

_____

_____

People that _____

_____

_____

_____

Pet peeves _____

_____

_____

_____

_____

Spirituality

As a child, my religious upbringing was _____

What I believe about god now is _____

_____

_____

_____

_____

My image of god is _____

_____

_____

_____

_____

Today my spiritual practice includes _____

_____

_____

_____

_____

Daily rituals I practice are _____

_____

_____

I also believe in _____

_____

_____

I plan to raise my children to believe that _____

_____

_____

I have _____ a mystical experience.

It was _____

_____

_____

_____

_____

The spiritual leaders (living or deceased) I would most like to meet are _____

_____

_____

_____

I believe that when you die you _____

_____

_____

Spirituality

When I die, I would like my funeral/memorial to _____

_____

_____

_____

_____

_____

I want to be _____ buried/ _____ cremated when I die

. . . and have my remains _____

_____

I am _____ organ donor

I have _____ made a last will

. . . and testament and you can find a copy of it _____

_____

My epitaph will read _____

_____

_____

_____

_____

_____

Dating

I _____ to be spontaneous.

The first thing that attracts me to someone is _____

_____

_____

The qualities I look for are _____

_____

_____

My idea of a great date is _____

_____

_____

_____

Other ideas for dates I would enjoy are _____

_____

_____

_____

_____

Videos/DVDs I like to rent on a date are _____

_____

_____

The kinds of dancing I like are _____

My views on double dating are _____

My views on blind dates are _____

Things I would not enjoy doing on a date are _____

Romance

I consider myself to be _____ romantic.

Romance is a _____ priority in my life.

My favorite time of day for romance is _____
_____

My idea of a romantic encounter is _____
_____
_____
_____
_____

One of my fantasies for a romantic night is to _____
_____
_____
_____

I think the most romantic place in the world is _____

The music that puts me in a romantic mood is _____
_____

The movies that put me in a romantic mood are _____

_____

_____

The following things put a damper on romance _____

_____

_____

_____

_____

My idea of a very romantic gift is _____

_____

_____

The least romantic gift I ever received from anyone was _____

_____

_____

The most romantic thing anyone has ever done for me was _____

_____

_____

_____

_____

When I ask for romance, what I really want is _____

_____

_____

_____

_____

_____

_____

_____

_____

_____

_____

The most significant romantic relationships in my life have been _____

_____

_____

_____

What really worked in my relationships in the past was _____

_____

_____

_____

_____

The former lover I would most like to know better is _____

   . . . because _____

_____

_____

The fairytale, which has most influenced my thinking about romance, was _____

_____

   . . . because _____

_____

_____

The songs and movies, which have most influenced my thinking about romance were _____

_____

_____

_____

_____

If a romantic relationship needed help, I would _____ be
willing to go to a couples counselor.

My position on monogamy is _____

_____

_____

Relationships

I _____ being in a committed relationship.

Most of my friends are _____ in a committed relationship.

My role models for relationships are _____

_____

_____

_____

The woman who has most influenced me in the area of a relationship was _____

_____

The man who has most influenced me was _____

_____

The longest platonic relationship I have had is _____

The longest romantic relationship I have had is _____

The recurring complaints I've had about relationships (romantic or platonic)

that I've been in are _____

_____

_____

_____

_____

_____

The recurring praises I've had about relationships (romantic or platonic) that I've been in are _____

_____

_____

_____

The lesson(s) I have learned from relationships _____

_____

_____

_____

The lesson(s) I still have to learn in relationships _____

_____

_____

_____

My parents are/were married for _____ years.

It was a _____ marriage.

How it affected me _____

_____

_____

_____

I can tolerate just about anything in a relationship except _____

_____

_____

If I had a crystal ball, I would predict that in five years _____

_____

_____

_____

I believe that pre-nuptial agreements are _____

_____

_____

_____

_____

My ideal wedding would be _____

_____

_____

_____

_____

_____

_____

Sex

I was _____ years old the first time I had sex.

The best part about it was _____

_____

The worst part was _____

_____

I think the three sexiest men on the planet today are _____

_____

_____

I think the three sexiest women on the planet today are _____

_____

_____

Someone I've always wanted to make love with is _____

The best sexual escapade I ever had was _____

_____

_____

_____

The worst was _____

_____

_____

Favorite positions _____

Least favorite _____

_____

Favorite locations _____

_____

Least favorite _____

_____

Favorite time of day to make love _____

Least favorite _____

Favorite lighting _____

Favorite music _____

Something I've always wanted to try and haven't is _____

Special things I really like _____

_____

_____

_____

Erogenous zones _____

_____

_____

_____

I am most in the mood for sex _____

_____

_____

Overall, I am _____ affectionate.

Public displays of affection make me _____

My favorite part of my body is _____

The part of my body I most like to have touched is _____

Kissing for me is like _____

_____

My ideal partner would like to have sex _____ times a _____

And it could take as long as _____

Sometimes I _____ a "quickie."

During sex I am _____

_____

I would describe my orgasms as _____

_____

_____

Immediately after orgasm I need you to _____

_____

After making love I like to _____

_____

Making love during menstruation _____

My favorite store to buy oils, lotions, and potions is _____

The type of sex that really turns me off is _____

_____

_____

_____

_____

_____

_____

Sexual Fantasies

I have always wanted to "do it" in the following places _____

_____

_____

_____

_____

_____

_____

_____

My top three sexual fantasies include _____

_____

_____

_____

_____

_____

_____

_____

_____

_____

_____

_____

Sex toys I enjoy are _____

_____

_____

The kinkiest thing I have ever done is _____

_____

_____

_____

_____

_____

I _____ enjoy sex with more than one partner.

If I knew someone was watching, I would _____

_____

I _____ dirty talk.

Holidays & Celebrations

My favorite holiday is _____

    . . . because _____

_____

How I like to spend:

    New Year's Eve _____

_____

_____

_____

_____

    Valentine's Day _____

_____

_____

_____

_____

    Easter/Passover _____

_____

_____

_____

_____

Mother's Day _____

_____

_____

_____

_____

Memorial Day weekend _____

_____

_____

Father's Day _____

_____

_____

Fourth of July _____

_____

_____

_____

_____

Labor Day _____

_____

_____

Halloween _____

_____

_____

Thanksgiving _____

_____

_____

Christmas/Hanukkah _____

_____

_____

_____

_____

My birthday _____

_____

My fantasy birthday celebration consists of _____

_____

_____

_____

_____

_____

Vacations & Travel

Types of vacations I prefer _____

_____

_____

_____

My dream vacation would include _____

_____

_____

_____

Ways I like to travel _____

_____

Places I want to see before I die _____

_____

_____

Places I have no desire to visit _____

_____

Most memorable childhood vacation _____

_____

_____

_____

Most memorable vacation as an adult _____

_____

_____

_____

If I took a long weekend, I would go to _____

_____

_____

_____

If I took a week or more, I would go to _____

_____

_____

_____

I _____ like to travel alone.

People I like to travel with are _____

_____

_____

_____

My Future

The basics I want for my life (marriage, children, etc.) include: _____

_____

_____

_____

My ideal house would be _____

_____

_____

_____

In five years I expect to be _____

_____

_____

_____

I plan to _____ working as soon as I am _____ years old.

My other ideas for a career include _____

_____

_____

_____

_____

_____

If I had to do it all over again, I would _____

_____

_____

_____

_____

_____

_____

_____

_____

In Case of Emergency

Please contact _____

    home phone _____

    mobile phone _____

    e-mail address _____

Someone in my office to contact _____

    office phone _____

My doctors are:

    medical: _____

        phone _____

    dentist: _____

        phone _____

    chiropractor: _____

        phone _____

    other doctor: _____

        phone _____

    other doctor: _____

        phone _____

    other doctor: _____

        phone _____

Miscellaneous phone numbers:

name: _____

    phone _____

name: _____

    phone _____

name: _____

    phone _____

name: _____

    phone _____

name: _____

    phone _____

name: _____

    phone _____

We hope this JODERE GROUP book has benefited you in your quest for personal, intellectual, and spiritual growth.

JODERE GROUP is passionate about bringing new and exciting books, such as Destructive Relationships, to readers worldwide. Our company was created as a unique publishing and multimedia avenue for individuals whose mission it is to positively impact the lives of others. We recognize the strength of an original thought, a kind word and a selfless act—and the power of the individuals who possess them. We are committed to providing the support, passion, and creativity necessary for these individuals to achieve their goals and dreams.

JODERE GROUP is comprised of a dedicated and creative group of people who strive to provide the highest quality of books, audio programs, online services, and live events to people who pursue life-long learning. It is our personal and professional commitment to embrace our authors, speakers, and readers with helpfulness, respect, and enthusiasm.

For more information about our products, authors, or live events, please call 800.569.1002 or visit us on the Web at www.jodere.com

JODERE
GROUP